Growing Readers

New Hanover County Public Library

Purchased with
New Hanover County Partnership for Children
and Smart Start Funds

Touching

By Sharon Gordon

Consultants
Nanci R. Vargus, Ed.D.
Primary Multiage Teacher
Decatur Township Schools, Indianapolis, Indiana

Jan Jenner, Ph.D.

Children's Press®
A Division of Scholastic Inc.
New York Toronto London Auckland Sydney
Mexico City New Delhi Hong Kong
Danbury, Connecticut

Designer: Herman Adler Design
Photo Researcher: Caroline Anderson
The photo on the cover shows two girls petting a rabbit.

Library of Congress Cataloging-in-Publication Data

Gordon, Sharon.
    Touching / by Sharon Gordon.
      p. cm. — (Rookie read-about health)
    Includes index.
    Summary: This simple introduction to the sense of touch discusses how
we feel things.
    ISBN 0-516-22290-2 (lib. bdg.)   0-516-25993-8 (pbk.)
    1. Touch—Juvenile literature. [1. Touch. 2. Senses and sensation.]
I. Title. II. Series.
QP451.G67   2001
612.8'8—dc21

                          00-057023

Touch the water.
Does it feel cool?

The sense of touch is one of the five senses. The others are seeing, hearing, smelling, and tasting.

You feel things with your skin. Skin covers almost all of your body.

You can feel things from your head to your toes!

Nerve endings in your skin tell your brain what you are touching.

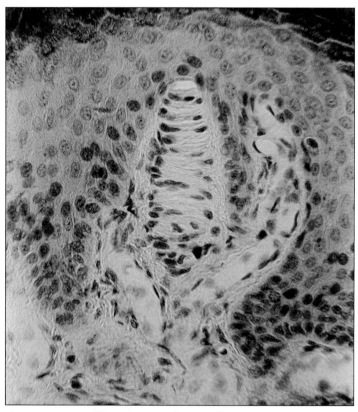

A nerve ending seen through a microscope

That is how you feel things.

Some places on your body have more nerve endings than others.

Your sense of touch is stronger in these areas, such as the bottoms of your feet.

Are you ticklish?

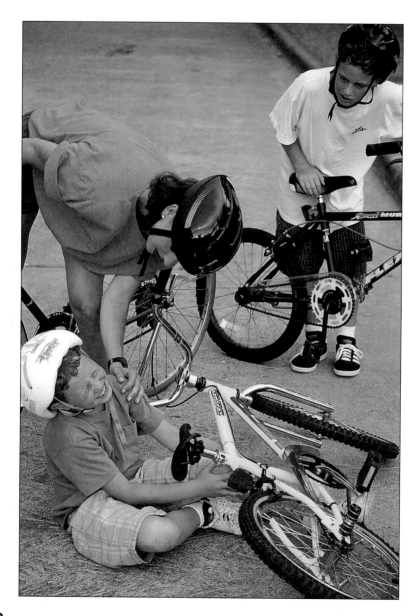

Your skin tells you about the things that touch your body. It tells you when something hurts.

Ouch! Be careful!

Try to make a snowball.
Your hands tell you the
snow is cold.

Put on some mittens first!

Go to the beach on
a sunny day. Your feet
feel the hot sand.

Your sense of touch
tells you to get to the
water—fast!

The sense of touch helps
you know when your
shoes are too small.

It tells you when you
have to scratch an itch.
That feels better!

You can feel many things
with your skin. You can
feel the shape of an object.

You can tell if something
is round or square.

You can tell if something
is hard or soft.

Some things are sharp to touch, such as the point of this pencil.

Some things are smooth,
such as marbles.

Close your eyes and guess
what you are touching now.

That's right—it is a soft and
furry kitten!

28

Did you ever touch
something sticky?

Pop!

29

Words You Know

kitten

marbles

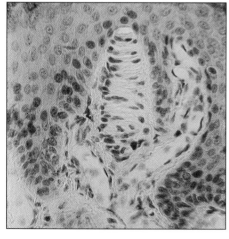

nerve ending

pencil

30

sand

skin

snowball

Index

beach, 17

body, 6, 13

brain, 8

cold, 14

cool, 3

feet, 10, 11, 17

five senses, 5

furry, 26, 27

hands, 14

hard, 22

head, 6

itch, 19

marbles, 25

nerve endings, 8, 10

pencil, 24

sand, 16, 17

shape, 20

sharp, 24

shoes, 18

skin, 6, 8, 13, 20

smooth, 25

snow, 14, 15

snowball, 14, 15

soft, 22, 23, 26, 27

sticky, 28, 29

toes, 6

water, 3, 17

About the Author

Sharon Gordon is a writer living in Midland Park, New Jersey. She and her husband have three school-aged children and a spoiled pooch. Together they enjoy visiting the Outer Banks of North Carolina as often as possible.

Photo Credits

Photographs ©: Peter Arnold Inc.: 15, 31 bottom (WHM Bildarchiv), 20 (Matt Meadows), 12 (Jim Olive), 8, 30 bottom left (J & L Weber); Photo Researchers, NY: 27, 30 top left (Richard Hutchings), 4 (Doug Martin); PhotoEdit: 22 (Jose Carrillo), 21 (M. K. Denny), 28 (Myrleen Ferguson), 23 (Kathy Ferguson-Johnson), 11, 19 (Richard Hutchings), 3, 9 (Michael Newman), 25, 30 top right (Jonathan Nourok); Rigoberto Quinteros: 18, 24, 30 bottom right; Stone: cover (David Oliver), 16, 31 top left (Darren Robb); Superstock, Inc.: 7, 31 top right.